On Acquisition of the Holy Spirit
Saint Seraphim of Sarov

Introduction

Saint Seraphim of Sarov was born in 1759, in city of Kursk. His parents were pious Orthodox Christians, examples of true spirituality. At the age of ten, Seraphim was miraculously healed from a serious illness by means of the Kursk icon of the Theotokos. As a boy, he immersed himself in church services and church literature. He began monastic life at the hermitage of Sarov at the age of nineteen. He was tonsured as a monk when he was twenty-seven, and soon afterwards was ordained a deacon. The intensity and purity of Seraphim's participation in the Divine services are evident as he was allowed to see angels, and during the liturgy on Holy

Thursday, he saw the Lord Himself.

At thirty-four, Seraphim was ordained as a priest, and was assigned as the spiritual guide of the Diveyevo convent. At this time, he also received a blessing to begin life as a hermit in the forest surrounding Sarov. He lived in a small cabin, devoting himself entirely to prayer, fasting, and the reading of the Scriptures and the Holy Fathers. Seraphim would go to the monastery on Sundays to receive Holy Communion; and then return to the forest.

In 1804, Seraphim was attacked by robbers and almost beaten to death. Permanent injuries sustained from this attack caused him to always be bent over and the need of a staff to walk. After this event, the Saint began more fervent prayers, incessant for a thousand days and a thousand nights; spending the better part of his time kneeling on a stone near his cell crying out, "Lord, be merciful to me, a sinner." Then he then spent three years in absolute silent seclusion. Obeying the request of the elders of the monastery, Seraphim returned to the monastery in 1810, but continued to live in prayer, and silent seclusion for another ten years. In obedience to a heavenly vision, Seraphim ended his silence and began to speak for the benefit of others. The Saint greeted all who came to him with a prostration, a kiss, and the words of the Pascha greeting: "Christ is Risen!" He called everyone, "my joy." In 1825, he returned to his forest cell, where he received thousands of pilgrims from across Russia. Granted the gift of clairvoyance, the wonder-working Saint Seraphim of Sarov gave consolation and guidance to all. Saint Seraphim died on January 2,

1833, while kneeling before an icon of the Theotokos.

An example of the grace of the Holy Spirit at work within the life and words of Saint Seraphim has been preserved for us. In November of 1831, a pious Orthodox Christian named Nicholas Motovilov met with Saint Seraphim, and recorded his conversation. The notes by Motovilov were transcribed and published by Sergius Nilus, who wrote the following introduction:

This revelation is undoubtedly of worldwide significance. True, there is nothing essentially new in it, for the full revelation was given to the Apostles from the very day of Pentecost. But now that people have forgotten the fundamental truths of Christian life and are immersed in the darkness of materialism or the exterior and routine performance of "ascetic labors," St. Seraphim's revelation is truly extraordinary, as indeed he himself regarded it.

"It is not given to you alone to understand this," said St. Seraphim towards the end of the revelation, "but through you it is for the whole world!" Like a flash of lightning this wonderful conversation illumined the whole world which was already immersed in spiritual lethargy and death less than a century before the struggle against Christianity in Russia and at a time when Christian faith was at a low ebb in the West. Here God's Saint appears before us in no way inferior to the prophets through whom the Holy Spirit Himself spoke.

We record everything word for word without any interpretations of our own.

On Acquisition of the Holy Spirit

S. A. Nilus

The Aim of the Christian Life

"It was Thursday," writes Motovilov. "The day was gloomy. The snow lay eight inches deep on the ground; and dry, crisp snowflakes were falling thickly from the sky when St. Seraphim began his conversation with me in a field near his hermitage, opposite the river Sarovka, at the foot of the hill which slopes down to the river bank. He sat me on the stump of a tree which he had just felled, and squatted opposite me.

"The Lord has revealed to me," said the great elder, "that in your

7

childhood you had a great desire
to know the aim of our Christian
life, and that you have continually
asked many great spiritual
persons about it."

I must admit, that from the age of
twelve this thought had constantly
troubled me. In fact, I had
approached many clergy about it,
however their answers had not
satisfied me. This could not have
been known to the elder.

"But no one,' continued St.
Seraphim, 'has given you a
precise answer. They have said to
you: "Go to church, pray to God,
do the commandments of God, do
good - that is the aim of the
Christian life." Some were even
indignant with you for being
occupied with such profane
curiosity and said to you, "Do not
seek things which are beyond
you." But they did not speak as
they should. Now humble

Seraphim will explain to you of what this aim really consists.

"However prayer, fasting, vigil and all the other Christian practices may be, they do not constitute the aim of our Christian life. Although it is true that they serve as the indispensable means of reaching this end, the true aim of our Christian life consists of the **acquisition of the Holy Spirit of God**. As for fasts, and vigils, and prayer, and almsgiving, and every good deed done for Christ's sake, are the only means of acquiring the Holy Spirit of God. Mark my words, only good deeds done for Christ's sake brings us the fruits of the Holy Spirit. All that is not done for Christ's sake, even though it be good, brings neither reward in the future life nor the grace of God in this life. That is why our Lord Jesus Christ said: "*He who does not gather with Me scatters*" (Luke 11:23). Not that a good deed can be called anything but gathering, even though a deed is not done for Christ's sake, it is still considered good. The Scriptures say: "*In every nation he who fears God and does what is right is acceptable to Him*" (Acts 10:35).

"As we see from another sacred narrative, the man who does what is right is pleasing to God. We see the Angel of the Lord appeared at the hour of prayer to Cornelius, the God-fearing and righteous centurion, and said: "Send to Joppa to Simon the Tanner; there you will find Peter and he will tell you the words of eternal life, whereby you will be saved and all your house." Thus the Lord uses all His divine means to give such a man, in return for his good works, the opportunity not to lose his reward in the future life. But to this end, we must begin with a right faith in our Lord Jesus Christ, the Son of God, Who came into the world to save sinners and Who, through our acquiring for ourselves the grace of the Holy Spirit, brings into our hearts the Kingdom of God and opens the way for us to win the blessings of the future life. But the acceptability to God of good deeds not done for Christ's sake is limited to this: the Creator gives the means to make them living (cf. Hebrews. 6:1). It rests with man to make them living or not. That is why the Lord said to the Jews: "*If you had been blind, you would have had no sin. But now you say 'We see,' so your sin remains*" (John 9:41). If a man like Cornelius enjoys the favor of God for his deeds, though not done for Christ's sake, and then believes in His Son, such deeds will be imputed to him as done for Christ's sake. But in the opposite event a man has no right to complain, when the good he has done is useless. It never is, when it is done for Christ's sake, since good done for Him not only merits a crown of righteousness in the world to come, but also in this present life fills us with the grace of the Holy Spirit. Moreover, it is said: "*God does not give the Spirit by measure*" (John 3:34-35).

"That is it, your Godliness. Acquiring the Spirit of God is the true aim of our Christian life, while prayer, fasting, almsgiving and other good works done for Christ's sake are merely **means** for acquiring the Spirit of God."

"What do you mean by acquiring?" I asked St. Seraphim. "Somehow I don't understand that."

"Acquiring is the same as obtaining," he replied. "Do you understand, what acquiring money means? Acquiring the Spirit of God is exactly the same. You know very well enough what it means to acquire in a worldly

12

sense, your Godliness. The aim of ordinary worldly people is to acquire or make money; and for the nobility, it is in addition to receive honors, distinctions and other rewards for their services to the government. The acquisition of God's Spirit is also capital, but grace-giving and eternal, and it is obtained in very similar ways, almost the same ways as monetary, social and temporal capital.

"God the Word, the God-Man, our Lord Jesus Christ, compares our life with the market, and the work of our life on earth He calls trading. He says to us all: *"Trade till I come"* (Lk. 19:13), "*buying up every opportunity, because the days are evil"* (Ephesians 5:16). In other words, make the most of your time getting heavenly blessings through earthly goods. Earthly goods are good works done for Christ's sake that confer the grace of the All-Holy Spirit, on us."

"In the parable of the wise and foolish virgins, when the foolish ones ran short of oil, they were told: "Go and buy in the market." But when they had bought it, the door of the bride-chamber was already shut and they could not get in. Some say that the lack of oil in the lamps of the foolish virgins means a lack of good deeds in their lifetime. Such an interpretation is not quite correct. Why should they be lacking in good deeds, if they are called virgins, even though foolish ones? Virginity is the supreme virtue, an angelic state, and it could take the place of all other good works.

"I think that what they were lacking was the grace of the All-Holy Spirit of God. These virgins practiced the virtues, but in their spiritual ignorance they supposed that the

14

Christian life consisted merely in doing good works. By doing a good deed they thought they were doing the work of God, but they cared little whether they acquired the grace of God's Spirit. These ways of life, based merely on doing good, without carefully testing whether they bring the grace of the Spirit of God, are mentioned in the patristic books: "There is another way which is deemed good in the beginning, but ends at the bottom of hell."

"Anthony the Great in his letters to monks says of such virgins: "Many monks and virgins have no idea of the different kinds of will which act in man, and they do not know that we are influenced by three wills: the first is God's all-perfect and all-saving will; the second is our own human will which, if not destructive, neither is it saving; and the third will is the devil's will - wholly destructive." This third will of the enemy prompts man to do any no good deeds, or to do them good out of vanity, or merely for virtue's sake rather than for Christ's sake. The second, our own will, prompts us to do everything to flatter our passions, or else it teaches us like the enemy, to do good for the sake of good and not care for the grace which is acquired by it. But the first, God's all-saving will, consists in doing good solely to acquire the Holy Spirit, as an eternal, inexhaustible treasure which is priceless. The acquisition of the Holy Spirit is, in a manner of speaking, the oil, which the foolish virgins lacked. They were called foolish just because they had forgotten the necessary fruit of virtue, the grace of the Holy Spirit, , without which no one is or can be saved, for: "Through the Holy Spirit every soul is quickened and through purification is exalted and illumined by the Triune Unity in a Holy mystery."

"The oil in the lamps of the wise virgins could burn brightly for a long time. So these virgins, with their bright lamps were able to meet the Bridegroom, who came at midnight. With Him, they could enter the bridal chamber of joy. But the foolish ones, though they went to market to buy more oil, when their lamps were going out, were unable to return in time, for the door was already shut. The market is our life; the door of the bridal chamber, which was shut and barred the way to the Bridegroom is human death; the wise and foolish virgins are Christian souls; the oil is not the good deeds, but the grace of the All-Holy Spirit of God which is obtained through good deeds and which changes souls from one state to another - such as, from a corruptible state to incorruptible

17

state, from spiritual death to spiritual life, from darkness to light, from the stable of our being (where the passions are tied up like dumb animals and wild beasts) into a temple of the Divinity, the shining bridal chamber of eternal joy in Christ Jesus our Lord, the Creator, Redeemer and eternal Bridegroom of our souls.

"How great is God's compassion on our misery, that is to say, our inattention to His care for us, when God says: *"Behold, I stand at the door and knock"* (Rev. 3:20), meaning by "*door*" the course of our life which has not yet been closed by death! Oh, how I wish, your Godliness, that in this life you may always be in the Spirit of God! "In whatsoever I find you, in that will I judge you," says the Lord.

"Woe betide us if He finds us overcharged with the cares and sorrows of this life! For who will be able to bear His anger, who will bear the wrath of His countenance? That is why it has been said: *"Watch and pray, lest you enter into temptation"* (Mk. 14:38), that is, lest you be deprived of the Spirit of God, for watching and prayer brings us His grace.

"Of course, every good deed done for Christ's sake gives us the grace of the Holy Spirit, but prayer gives us this grace most of all, for it is always at hand, as an instrument for acquiring the grace of the Spirit. For instance, you would like to go to church, but there is no church or the service is over; you would like to give alms to a beggar, but there isn't one, or you have nothing to give; you would like to preserve your virginity, but you have not the

19

strength to do so because of your temperament, or because of the violence of the wiles of the enemy which because of your human weakness you cannot withstand; you would like to do some other good deed for Christ's sake, but either you have not the strength or the opportunity is lacking. This certainly does not apply to prayer. Prayer is always possible for everyone, rich and poor, noble and humble, strong and weak, healthy and sick, righteous and sinful.

"You may judge how great the power of prayer is even in a sinful person, when it is offered whole-heartedly, by the' following example from Holy Tradition. When at the request of a desperate mother who had been deprived by death of her only son, a harlot whom she chanced to meet, still unclean from her last sin, and who was touched by the mother's deep sorrow, cried to the

Lord: "Not for the sake of a wretched sinner like me, but for the sake of the tears of a mother grieving for her son and firmly trusting in Thy loving kindness and Thy almighty power, Christ God, raise up her son, O Lord!" And the Lord raised him up.

"You see, your Godliness! Great is the power of prayer, and it brings most of all the Spirit of God, and is most easily practiced by everyone. We shall be happy indeed if the Lord God finds us watchful and filled with the gifts of His Holy Spirit. Then we may boldly hope *"to be caught up . . . in the clouds to meet the Lord in the air"* (1 Thess. 4:17) Who is coming *"with great power and glory"* (Mk. 13:26) *"to judge the living and the dead"* (1 Peter 4:5) and *"to reward every man according to his works"* (Matt. 16:27).

"Your Godliness deigns to think it a great happiness to talk to poor Seraphim, believing that even he is not bereft of the grace of the Lord. What then shall we say of the Lord Himself, the never-failing source of every blessing both heavenly and earthly? Truly in prayer we are granted to converse with Him, our all-gracious and life-giving God and Savior Himself. But even here we must pray only until God the Holy Spirit descends on us in measures of His heavenly grace known to Him. <u>And when He deigns to visit us, we must stop praying.</u> Why should we then pray to Him, "Come and abide in us and cleanse us from all impurity and save our souls, O Good One," when He has already come to us to save us, who trust in Him, and truly call on His holy Name, that humbly and lovingly we may receive Him, the Comforter, in the mansions of our souls, hungering and thirsting for His coming?

"I will explain this point to your Godliness through an example. Imagine that you have invited me to pay you a visit, and at your invitation I come to have a talk with you. But you continue to invite me, saying: "Come in, please. Do come in!" Then I should be obliged to think: "What is the matter with him? Is he out of his mind?"

"So it is with regard to our Lord God the Holy Spirit. That is why it is said: *"Be still and know that I am God; I will be exalted among the nations. I will be exalted in the earth"* (Ps. 45[46]:10). That is, I will appear and will continue to appear to everyone who believes in Me and calls upon Me, and I will converse with him as once I conversed with Adam in Paradise, with Abraham and Jacob and other servants of Mine, with Moses and Job, and those like them.

Many explain that this stillness refers only to worldly matters; in other words, that during prayerful converse with God you must "be still" with regard to worldly affairs. But I will tell you in the name of God that not only is it necessary to be dead to them at prayer, but when by the omnipotent power of faith and prayer our Lord God the Holy Spirit condescends to visit us, and comes to us in the plenitude of His unutterable goodness, we must be dead to prayer too.

"The soul speaks and converses during prayer, but at the descent of the Holy Spirit we must remain in complete silence, in order to hear clearly and intelligibly all the words of eternal life which he will then deign to communicate. Complete soberness of soul and spirit, and chaste purity of body is required at the same time. The same demands were made at

24

Mount Horeb, when the Israelites were told not even to touch their wives for three days before the appearance of God on Mount Sinai. For our God is a fire which consumes everything unclean, and no one who is defiled in body or spirit can enter into communion with Him."

The Acquisition of Grace

"Yes, father, but what about other good deeds done for Christ's sake in order to acquire the grace of the Holy Spirit? You have only been speaking of prayer."

"Acquire the grace of the Holy Spirit also by practicing all the other virtues for Christ's sake. Trade spiritually with them; trade with those which give you the greatest profit. Accumulate capital from the superabundance of God's grace, deposit it in God's eternal bank which will bring you immaterial interest, not four or six

26

per cent, but one hundred per cent for one spiritual ruble, and even infinitely more than that. For example, if prayer and watching gives you more of God's grace, watch and pray; if fasting gives you much of the spirit of God, fast; if almsgiving gives you more, give alms. Weigh every virtue done for Christ's sake in this manner.

"Now I will tell you about myself, poor Seraphim. I come of a merchant family in Kursk. So when I was not yet in the monastery we used to trade with the goods which brought us the greatest profit. Act like that, my son. And just as in business the main point is not merely to trade, but to get as much profit as possible, so in the business of the Christian life the main point is not merely to pray or to do some other good deed. Though the apostle says: "*Pray without ceasing*" (1 Thess. 5:17), yet, as you remember, he adds: "*I would rather speak five words with my understanding than ten thousand words with a tongue"* (1 Cor. 14:19). And the Lord says: *"Not everyone who says to Me: Lord, Lord,* shall be saved, *but he who does the will of My Father"* (Mt. 7:21), that is he who does the work of God and, moreover, does it with reverence, for *"cursed is he who does the work of God negligently"* (Jer. 48:10). And the work of God is: believe in God and in Him Whom He has sent, Jesus Christ (John 14:1; 6:29). If we understand the commandments of Christ and of the Apostles aright, our business as Christians consists not in increasing the number of our good deeds which are only the means of furthering the purpose of our Christian life, but in deriving from them the utmost profit, that is in acquiring the most abundant gifts of the Holy Spirit.

"How I wish, your Godliness, that you yourself may acquire this inexhaustible source of divine grace, and may always ask yourself: Am I in the Spirit of God, or not? - there is nothing to grieve about. You are ready to appear before the awful judgment of Christ immediately. For "In whatsoever I find you, in that will I judge you." But if we are not in the Spirit, we must discover why not and what reason our Lord God the Holy Spirit has willed to abandon us. We must seek Him again and must go on searching until our Lord God the Holy Spirit has been found and is with us again, through His goodness. We must attack the enemies that drive us away from Him until even their dust is no more, as the Prophet David has said, *"I will pursue my enemies and overtake them; and I will not turn back till they are destroyed. I will crush them and they will be unable to stand; they*

29

will fall under my feet" (Ps. 17[18]: 38-39)."

"That's it, my son. That is how you must spiritually trade in virtue. Distribute the Holy Spirit's gifts of grace to those in need of them, just as a lighted candle burning with earthly fire shines itself and lights other candles for the illumining of all in other places, without diminishing its own light. If it is so, with regard to the earthly fire, what shall we say about the fire of the grace of the All-Holy Spirit of God? For earthly riches decrease with distribution, but the more the heavenly riches of God's grace are distributed, the more they increase in the one who distributes them. Thus the Lord Himself was pleased to say to the Samaritan woman: *All who drink this water will be thirsty again. "But whoever drinks the water that I shall give him will never be thirsty any more; but the water that I shall give him will be in him a spring of water leaping up to eternal life"* (John 4:13-14)."

The Presence of the

Holy Spirit in History

"Father," said I, "you speak all the time of the acquisition of the grace of the Holy Spirit as the aim of the Christian life. But how and where can I see it? Good deeds are visible, but can the Holy Spirit be seen? How am I to know whether He is with me or not?"

"At the present time," the elder replied, "Owing to our almost universal coldness to our holy faith

32

in our Lord Jesus Christ, and our inattention to the working of His Divine Providence in us, and to the communion of man with God, we have gone so far that, one may say, we have almost abandoned the true Christian life. The testimonies of Holy Scripture now seem strange to us; when, for instance, by the lips of Moses the Holy Spirit says: "And Adam saw the Lord walking in Paradise" (cf. Gen. 3:10), or when we read the words of the Apostle Paul: "We went to Achaia, and the Spirit of God went not with us; we returned to Macedonia, and the Spirit of God came with us." More than once in other passages of Holy Scripture the appearance of God to men is mentioned.

"That is why some people say: "These passages are incomprehensible. Is it really possible for people to see God so openly?" But there is nothing incomprehensible here. This failure to understand has come about because we have departed from the simplicity of the original Christian knowledge. Under the pretext of education, we have reached such a darkness of ignorance, that the things the ancients understood so clearly, seem to us almost inconceivable. Even in ordinary conversation, the idea of God's appearance among men did not seem strange to them. Thus, when his friends rebuked him for blaspheming God, Job answered them: "How can that be when I feel the Spirit of God in my nostrils?" (cf. Job 27:3). That is, "How can I blaspheme God when the Holy Spirit abides with me? If I had blasphemed God, the Holy Spirit would have withdrawn from me; but look! I feel His breath in my nostrils."

"It is said that Abraham and Jacob saw the Lord and conversed with

Him in exactly the same way, and that Jacob even wrestled with Him. Moses and all the people with him saw God, when he received the tablets of the law on Mount Sinai from God. A pillar of cloud and a pillar of fire, or in other words, the evident grace of the Holy Spirit, served as guides to God's people in the desert. People saw God and the grace of His Holy Spirit not during sleep, in dreams, or in the excitement of a disordered imagination, but truly and openly.

"We have become so inattentive to the work of our salvation, that we misinterpret many other words in Holy Scripture as well, all because we do not seek the grace of God and in the pride of our minds, do not allow it to dwell in our souls. That is why we are without true enlightenment from the Lord, which He sends into the hearts of men who hunger and thirst wholeheartedly for God's righteousness or holiness."

Many explain the part in the Bible, *"God breathed the breath of life into the face of Adam"* the first-created, who was created by Him from the dust of the ground, it must mean that until that moment there was neither human soul nor spirit in Adam, but only the flesh created from the dust of the ground. This interpretation is wrong, for the Lord created Adam from the dust of the ground with the constitution which the holy Apostle Paul describes: *"May your spirit and soul and body be preserved blameless at the coming of our Lord Jesus Christ"* (1 Thess. 5:23). And all these parts of our nature were created from the dust of the ground, and Adam was not created dead, but an active being like all of God's animate creatures living on earth.

36

The point is, that if the Lord God had not breathed afterwards into his face, this *breath of life* - that is, the **grace** of our Lord God the Holy Spirit Who proceeds from the Father, rests in the Son and is sent into the world for the Son's sake - Adam would have remained without the Holy Spirit within him. It is the Holy Spirit who raised Adam to Godlike dignity. However perfect, he had been created and superior to all the other creatures of God, as the crown of creation on earth, he would have been just like all the other creatures, though they have a body, soul and spirit, each according to its kind, do not have the Holy Spirit within them. But when the Lord God breathed into Adam's face the breath of life, then, according to Moses' word, *"Adam became a living soul"* (Gen. 2:7), that is, completely and in every-way like God, and like Him, forever immortal. Adam was immune to the action of the elements to such a degree that water could not drown him, fire could not burn him, the earth could not swallow him in its abysses, and the air could not harm him by any kind of action whatever. Everything was subject to him as the beloved of God, as the king and lord of creation, and everything looked up to him, as the perfect crown of God's creatures. Adam was made so wise by this breath of life, which was breathed into his face from the creative lips of God, the Creator and Ruler of all, that there has never been a man on earth wiser or more intelligent, and it is unlikely that there ever will be. When the Lord commanded him to give names to all the creatures, he gave every creature a name which completely expressed all the qualities, powers and properties given it by God at its creation.

"As a result of this gift, of the supernatural grace of God, which was infused into him by the breath of life, Adam could see, understand the Lord walking in Paradise, comprehend His words, understand the conversation of the holy Angels, the language of all beasts, birds and reptiles and all that is now hidden from us the fallen and sinful creatures. All this was so clear to Adam before his fall. The Lord God also gave Eve the same wisdom, strength, unlimited power, and all the other good and holy qualities. He created her not from the dust of the ground, but from Adam's rib in the Eden of delight, the Paradise which He had planted in the midst of the earth.

"In order that they might always easily maintain the immortal, divine and perfect properties of this breath of life, God planted in the midst of the garden the *tree of life* with fruits endowed with all the essence and fullness of His divine breath. If they had not sinned, Adam and Eve themselves as well as all their posterity could have always eaten of the fruit of the tree of life and so would have eternally maintained the vivifying power of divine grace.

"They could have also maintained for all eternity the full powers of their body, soul and spirit in a state of immortality and perpetual youth, and they could have continued in this immortal and blessed state of theirs forever. At the present time, however, it is difficult for us even to imagine such grace.

"But through the tasting of the tree of the knowledge of good and evil - which was premature and contrary to the commandment of God - they learnt the difference between good and evil and were subjected to all the afflictions

40

which followed the transgression of the commandment of God. Then they lost this priceless gift of the grace of the Spirit of God, so that, until the actual coming into the world of the God-man Jesus Christ, *"the Spirit of God was not yet* in the world *because Jesus was not yet glorified"* (John 7:39).

"However, that does not mean that the Spirit of God was not in the world at all, but His presence was not so apparent. It manifested only externally, and only the signs of His presence in the world were known to mankind. Thus, for instance, many mysteries in connection with the future salvation of the human race were revealed to Adam as well as to Eve after their fall. For Cain, in spite of his impiety and his transgression, it was easy for him to understand the voice which held grace and divinity, though convicting words. Noah conversed with God. Abraham saw God and His day and was glad (from John 8:56). The grace of the Holy Spirit acting externally was also reflected in all the Old Testament prophets and saints of Israel. Afterwards, the Hebrews established special prophetic schools where the sons of the prophets were taught to discern the signs of the manifestation of God or Angels, and to distinguish the operations of the Holy Spirit from the ordinary natural phenomena of graceless earthly life. Simeon who held God in his arms, Christ's grandparents Joachim and Anna, and countless other servants of God continually often had various divine apparitions, revelations and heard voices, which were corroborated by evident miraculous events. Though not with the same power as in the people of God, nevertheless the presence of the Spirit of God also acted in the pagans who did not know the true God, because even among them, God found the chosen people. For instance, there were the virgin-prophetesses called Sibyls who vowed virginity to an unknown God, but to God, the Creator of the universe, the all-powerful ruler of the world, as He was conceived by the pagans. Though the pagan philosophers also wandered in the darkness of ignorance of God, yet they sought the truth which is beloved by God. Because of this, God-pleasing seeking, they could partake of the Spirit of God. It is said, that nations who do not know God, practice by nature the demands of the law and do what is pleasing to God (cf. Rom. 2:14). The Lord so praises truth that He says of it Himself by the Holy Spirit: "*Truth has sprung from the earth, and justice has looked down from heaven*" (Ps. 84[85]:11).

"So you see, your Godliness, both in the holy Hebrew people, a people beloved by God, and in the pagans who did not know God, there was preserved a knowledge of God - thus, my son, a clear and rational comprehension of how our Lord God the Holy Spirit acts in man, and by means of our inner and outer feelings, one can be sure that this is really the action of our Lord God the Holy Spirit, and not a delusion of the enemy. That is how it was, from Adam's fall, until the coming into the world of the Lord Jesus Christ, in the flesh.

"Without this perceptible realization of the actions of the Holy Spirit which had always been preserved in human nature, men could not have possibly known for certain whether the fruit of the seed of the woman who had been promised to Adam and Eve had come into the world to crush the serpent's head (Gen. 3:15).

"At last the Holy Spirit foretold to St. Simeon, who was then in his 65th year, the mystery of the virginal conception and birth of Christ from the most pure Ever-Virgin Mary. Afterwards, having lived by the grace of the All-Holy Spirit of God for three hundred years, in the 365th year of his life he said openly in the temple of the Lord that he knew for certain through the gift of the Holy Spirit that this was that very Christ, the Savior of the world, Whose supernatural conception and birth from the Holy Spirit had been foretold to him by an Angel three hundred years previously.

And there was also St. Anna, a prophetess, the daughter of Phanuel, who from her widowhood had served the Lord God in the temple of God for eighty years, and who was known to be a righteous widow, a chaste servant of God, from the special gifts of grace which she had received. She too announced that He was actually the Messiah Who had been promised to the world, the true Christ, God and Man, the King of Israel, Who had come to save Adam and mankind.

"But when our Lord Jesus Christ accomplished the whole work of salvation, after His Resurrection, He breathed on the Apostles, restored the breath of life lost by Adam, and gave them the same grace of the All-Holy Spirit of God as Adam had enjoyed. But that was not all. He also told them that it was better for them that He should go to the Father, for if He did not go, the Spirit of God would not come into the world. But if He, the Christ, went to the Father, He would send Him into the world, and He, the Comforter, would guide them and all who followed their teaching into all truth and would remind them of all that He

46

had said to them when He was still in the world. What was then promised was *"grace upon grace"* (John 1:16).

"Then on the day of Pentecost He solemnly sent down to them in a tempestuous wind the Holy Spirit in the form of tongues of fire which alighted on each of them and entered within them and filled them with the fiery strength of divine grace which breathes as with dew and acts with gladness in souls who partake of its power and operations (Acts ch. 2). And this same fire-infusing grace of the Holy Spirit which is given to us all, the faithful in Christ, in the Sacrament of Holy Baptism, is sealed by the Sacrament of Chrismation on the chief parts of our body as appointed by the Holy Church, the eternal keeper of this grace. It is said: "The seal of the gift of the Holy Spirit." On what do we put our seals, your Godliness, if not on vessels containing some very precious treasure? But what on earth can be higher and what can be more precious than the gifts of the Holy Spirit which are sent down to us from above in the Sacrament of Holy Baptism? This baptismal grace is so great and so indispensable, so vital for man, that even a heretic is not deprived of it until his actual death; that is, till the end of the period appointed on high by the providence of God as a lifelong test of man on earth, in order to see what he will be able to achieve (during this period given to him by God) by means of the power of grace granted to him from on high.

"And if we were never to sin after our baptism, we should remain for ever saints of God, holy, blameless, and free from all impurity of body and spirit. But the trouble is that we increase in stature, but do not increase in grace and in the knowledge of God as our Lord Jesus Christ increased; but on the contrary, we gradually become more and more depraved and lose the grace of the All-Holy Spirit of God and become sinful in various degrees, and very sinful people. But if a man is stirred by the wisdom of God, which seeks our salvation and embraces everything, and if he is resolved for its sake to devote the early hours of the day to God and to watch in order to find His eternal salvation, then, in obedience to its voice, he must hasten to offer true repentance for all his sins and must practice the virtues which are opposite to the sins committed. Then through the virtues practiced for Christ's sake, he will acquire the Holy Spirit Who acts within us and establishes in us the Kingdom of God. The word of God does not say in vain: *"The Kingdom of God is within you"* (Luke 17:21), and it *"suffers violence, and the violent take it by force"* (Matt. 11:12). That means that people who, in spite of the bonds of sin which fetter them and (by their violence and by inciting them to new sins) prevent them from coming to Him, our Savior, with perfect repentance for reckoning with Him. They force themselves to break their bonds, despising all the strength of the fetters of sin - such people at last actually appear before the face of God made whiter than snow by His grace. *"Come, says the Lord: Though your sins be as purple, I will make you white as snow"* (Is. 1:18).

"Such people were once seen by the holy Seer John the Divine *clothed in white robes* (that is, in robes of justification) and with *palms in their hands* (as a sign of victory), and they were singing to God a wonderful song: *Alleluia.* And no one could imitate the beauty of their song. Of them an Angel of God said: *"These are they who have come out of the great tribulation and have washed their robes, and have made them white in the blood of the Lamb"* (Rev. 7:9-14). They were washed with their sufferings and made white in the communion of the immaculate and life-giving Mysteries of the Body and Blood of the most pure and spotless Lamb - Christ - Who was slain before all ages by His own will for the salvation of the world, and Who is continually being slain and divided until now, but is never exhausted (in the Sacrament of Communion). Through the Holy Mysteries we are granted our eternal and unfailing salvation as a viaticum to eternal life, as an acceptable answer at His dread judgment and a precious substitute beyond our comprehension for that fruit of the tree of life of which the enemy of mankind, Lucifer, who fell from heaven, would have liked to deprive the human race. Though the enemy and devil seduced Eve, and Adam fell with her, yet the Lord not only granted them a Redeemer in the fruit of the seed of the woman Who trampled down death by death, but also granted us all in the woman, the Ever-Virgin Mary Mother of God, who crushes the head of the serpent in herself and in all the human race, a constant mediatress with her Son and our God, and an invincible and persistent intercessor even for the most desperate sinners. That is why the Mother of God is called the "Plague of Demons," for it is not possible for a devil to destroy a man so long as man himself has recourse to the help of the Mother of God.

Grace is Light

"And I must further explain, your Godliness, the difference between the operations of the Holy Spirit Who dwells mystically in the hearts of those who believe in our Lord God and Savior Jesus Christ and the operations of the darkness of sin which at the suggestion and instigation of the devil, acts predatorily in us. The Spirit of God reminds us of the words of our Lord Jesus Christ and always acts triumphantly with Him, gladdening our hearts and guiding our steps into the way of peace, while the false, diabolical spirit reasons in the opposite way to Christ, and its actions in us are rebellious, stubborn, and full of the lust of the flesh, the lust of the eyes and the pride of life.

"And whoever lives and believes in Me will never die" (John 11:26). He who has the grace of the Holy Spirit in reward for right faith in Christ, even if on account of human frailty his soul were to die for some sin or other, yet he will not die for ever, but he will be raised by the grace of our Lord Jesus Christ *"Who takes away the sin of the world"* (John 1:29), and freely gives grace upon grace. Of this grace, which was manifested to the whole world and to our human race by the God-man, it is said in the Gospel: *"In Him was life, and the life was the light of men"* (John 1:4); and further: *"And the light shines in the darkness; and the darkness has never swallowed it"* (John 1:5). This means that the grace of the Holy Spirit which is granted at baptism in the name of the Father and the Son and the Holy Spirit, in spite of man's fall into sin, in spite of the darkness surrounding our soul,

nevertheless shines in our hearts with the divine light (which has existed from time immemorial) of the inestimable merits of Christ. In the event of a sinner's impenitence this light of Christ cries to the Father: "Abba, Father! Be not angry with this impenitence to the end (of his life)." Then, at the sinners conversion to the way of repentance, it effaces completely all trace of past sin and clothes the former sinner once more in a robe of incorruption spun from the grace of the Holy Spirit. The acquisition of this is the aim of the Christian life, which I have been explaining to your Godliness.

"I will tell you something else, so that you may understand more clearly what is meant by the grace of God, how to recognize it and how its action is manifested particularly in those who are enlightened by it. The grace of the Holy Spirit is the light which enlightens man. The whole of Sacred Scripture speaks about this. Thus our Holy Father David said: *"Thy law is a lamp to my feet, and a light to my paths"* (Ps. 118[119]:105), and *"Unless Thy law had been my meditation, I should have died in my humiliation"* (Ps. 118[119]:92). In other words, the grace of the Holy Spirit which is expressed in the Law, by the words of the Lord's commandments, is my lamp and light. If this grace of the Holy Spirit (which I try to acquire so carefully and zealously that I meditate on Thy just judgments seven times a day) did not enlighten me amidst the darkness of the cares which are inseparable from the high calling of my royal rank, whence should I get a spark of light to illumine my way on the path of life, which is darkened by the ill-will of my enemies?

"In fact the Lord has frequently demonstrated before many witnesses how the grace of the Holy Spirit acts on people whom He has sanctified and illumined by His great inspirations. Remember Moses after his talk with God on Mount Sinai. He so shone with an extraordinary light that people were unable to look at him. He was even forced to wear a veil when he appeared in public. Remember the Transfiguration of the Lord on Mount Tabor. A great light encircled Him, *"and His raiment became shining, exceedingly white like snow"* (Mk. 9:3), and His disciples fell on their faces from fear. But when Moses and Elijah appeared to Him in that light, a cloud overshadowed them in order to hide the radiance of the light of the divine grace which blinded the eyes of the disciples. Thus the grace of the All-Holy Spirit of God appears in an ineffable light to all to whom God reveals its action."

Made in the USA
Columbia, SC
30 September 2020